HORIZON NOTE

*Also by Robin Behn*

PAPER BIRD

THE OBOIST *(limited edition)*

THE RED HOUR

THE PRACTICE OF POETRY:
WRITING EXERCISES FROM
POETS WHO TEACH *(co-editor)*

# HORIZON NOTE ❦ Robin Behn

THE UNIVERSITY OF WISCONSIN PRESS

The University of Wisconsin Press
1930 Monroe Street
Madison, Wisconsin 53711

www.wisc.edu/wisconsinpress/

3 Henrietta Street
London WC2E 8LU, England

5    4    3    2    1

Printed in Canada

Library of Congress Cataloging-in-Publication Data
Behn, Robin.
    Horizon note / Robin Behn.
    pp.   cm. — (The Brittingham prize in poetry)
    ISBN 0-299-17534-0 (cloth: alk. paper)
    ISBN 0-299-17530-8 (pbk.: alk. paper)
    1. Parent and child—Poetry.
  I. Title. II. Brittingham prize in poetry (Series)
  PS3552.E412 H67   2001
  811'.54—dc21   2001002082

This is my Father's world,
and to my listening ears
all nature sings, and round me rings
the music of the spheres.

*for Stephen and Simon*

CONTENTS

ACKNOWLEDGMENTS

Many thanks to the MacDowell Colony, the Ragdale Foundation, and the Vermont Studio Center; to the John Simon Guggenheim Foundation, the National Endowment for the Arts, and the University of Alabama College of Arts and Sciences and Research Advisory Committee; and to Bruce Smith, Deborah Digges, and Clare Rossini.

Thanks to the editors of the magazines in which the following poems previously appeared, sometimes in different versions:

*American Literary Review*: "Elegy for the Difference Between Reading and Being"
*Bellingham Review*: "Vigil: Dwindle," "Postlude for Penny Whistle, Spoons, and Drum"
*Chelsea*: "The Primary Tool Is Soup"
*Colorado Review*: "The Difference Between Writing and Music"
*Crab Orchard Review*: "Ark," "Interlude: Still Still," "To Brain on Brain's Last Day as Brain"
*Field*: "Slide," "The Scientist," "Sylvia's Starlings," "The Swim," "On Giving My Father a Book About Roses"
*The Iowa Review*: "On Being Asked My Opinion About an Autopsy," "Prelude for Penny Whistle"
*Kenyon Review*: "Elegy for Lessons," "Ballad in Fall," "Whether or Not There Are Apples," "Still Life"
*Luna*: "On Being Asked About Giving Up the Flute"
*New Letters*: "The Other Side," "Wolf Story"
*Southern Review*: "Double Elegy in Spring"
*Spoon River Poetry Review*: "On Thursday She Began Saying Everything at Once"
*Third Coast*: "The Call"

"Slide" also appeared in *Poetry Daily* (www.poems.com).
"On Giving My Father a Book About Roses" also appeared in *The Red Hour*.

# Prelude for Penny Whistle

—FOR D.


Since then, no day is silent, or only a rare day
has enough forgetting in it to be silent
enough to keep me from calling you
back up out of water or sunlight.

I have a bridge but it is not the one
you stepped from. Nor the one
you used to move from key to key.

I learned it
from the spider who expresses
her beautiful hunger in one strand.

If you play the fat black note of her body
anywhere upon her intricate staff
it only sounds like her.

And her and her.

And her-and-her-and-her.

Other notes she handily
devours in their brief casings.
And so she has no *you*
that lasts. But still she hungers.

Subject, you are subject
to these spinning whims
because you will not leave
and because you will not fill me.

Mind, our favorite house,
is just a kind of body, not,
as you thought, a body
of thought
that reaches the utter end
of sucked-back silk.

You'll feel it, this spin.
(Forced grin.)
Let's begin
to tinker on your old tin
whistle with a tune:

Water and sunlight.
Water and cloudlight.
Water and dark.
Dry dark. Dry dock.

Tick tock.
Dark clock.
It's time
you knocked.

# Still Life

There is a train, no, there are train
tracks wrapped around the cliff and
the train and its
I'm-about-to-take-him-off-to-war.

They stroll, the two of them.
I've decided they shall stroll:
slowly, tie to tie,
over cinders, river, cinders, air,

zipping up the distance
with their four fine shoes,
my mother's, a little worn,
as she's saving her coupons for skates.

Right/right, left/left, destiny
clops. She, why not, in, why not, blue
dotted Swiss like a pointillist's try at sky,
a dash of pigment pink on the one cheek that shows.

Her suitor's, no, teacher's, no, suitor's
—she's just graduated!—face
happens (no photos) to be hidden
completely by the shadow of the cliff.

But here in the conjured light,
she wraps her elbow
through his proffered elbow
and the fleshy double helix

floats dreamily round the bend
into the darling future the train
gobbles, smacking them
against the cliff face like a kiss.

—We almost died, she told a brother who half
a century later told me,
but what could it matter now,
her happiness almost ending a few weeks sooner than it did?

War is just one kind of dare.
Maybe we get our first loves
and maybe we get our second loves,
but what do we tell our hearts,

cropped crooked as practice valentines,
still bloodily bleating on some cliff?
After my father goes off
*First you must let go*

to the war in his brain,
*and then there is this terrible embracing.*
my mother takes up painting.
Flower's faces. Vases and vases.

# On Being Asked My Opinion About an Autopsy

Wherever I am, now, I'm braced:
my mother announcing your release
into the serum of bright light
your brain had begun to be bathed in in this life
—she will not say it that way.
No one, don't worry, will say it that way.

Nor how every Sunday of your unravaged life
you walked alone down three steps,
closed the door behind you and typed,
on and off, your one-note hymn
in which—forgive me, you never said what
should happen to the files—
a raven-haired woman
walked the streets of New York, her long legs flashing
in the web of tangled traffic as you tried to follow her . . .

Books call it *tangles* and *plaques*.
So it seems you got it right, the mind
the woman walked in. And, empty spaces surrounding
*densely shaped granules of unknown significance*
in the part, get this, named for its *seahorse* shape that's
memory's storehouse. Though no doubt you'd favor
the Greek *hippo/campus*—some fat, gray-faced new kid
you'd stick in the front row, extract
recitations from, including (he'd know it of course)
certain choice passages from *The Great Unpublished American Novel*—

Call me to task on that one.
Make me pay. Make me stay after school.
Make me feel what it's like after-hours.

How quiet quiet is, how hushed the hallowed halls,
who's sweeping up the bundles, recording
shrinkage, erasing *Mr.* from *Behn* and clapping
huge clouds of him against the brick building
till great, pocked, rectangular hoof marks mark
where something trapped stamps till the ground
goes white with the sound of its passing, almost passing,
but *something*, still pacing, majestic, heart-high:

I will not let them hunt you down after you've gone.
I will not let them break the binding,
I will not let them leaf through the brain,
older now, and withered, and bound
to what's called *tracks*.

# A Brief History of Music

The piano was not right
about chords of black and white.

Notes were all the same
or all different colors, a murk

except for C,
life's most apparent key.

She quit. But that was later.
This time she quit piano.

Which opened up a place in which birds
could cry out one at a time

—next-, next-next-next—
like landing lights leading

down a corridor in space,
forward, forever, flute.

But, the double-cross
of having to double back.

Of try-again. Of take-it-from-the-top.
Of this-time,-please,-with-feeling.

The music stand's three disappearing legs.
The fat spider tangled in webs of arpeggios

drawing up its legs into the whole-note
stupor of whole afternoons.

Broken by double-tonguing.
Surrounded by circular breathing.

By overtones—hypnotic, hydraulic—
percussive key strokes, bass notelessnesses,

by the god-throat itself pinched sometimes
to a piccolo or swelled up to bass flute—

Things in her sleep.
Clefs uncurving.

The staff's five sunken highways and the floating
scars of ledger lines like handholds

on a mountain that ascends past sky
into the face, the faces, yes, of lace, was how, yes,

the teacher was saying it, holding her elbows,
breathing when she breathed

until sound was transmogrified
back into the glory of flesh.

Indeed.
In deed.

Flesh, of course, drew back
into its swirl of slow silence.

But words, *his* words,
*lace,* yes, *faceless,* had

a grace inside that shone silence open
like a flashlight through dense smoke

—the light
being anyone's now,

the smoke being anyone's
anything now, the place

art comes from
being the place

to which, for which, from which
*listen:*

*next-,*
*next-next-next:*

the first bird tests the morning
to see if it is there

and because it is there
is good

*and because    it is*
*there is good.*

# Early Instance

Once, the violin maker bent
so close and for so long to beauty
he almost saw the saw as it ravished his hand.

But now, his three fingers light upon her face
—here-, here-here-here—
amid the forest of primitive instruments

—horn and crumhorn, lute and three-holed flute—
branching from hooks along the walls
of his one room.

This maker makes her sad.
Or good. Or safe. Or steady.
Or briefly steadfast in his birdfoot hand.

And after, since she asks,
he plays one of his fiddles for her,
tucking it under his right ear,

bowing with what is left of his left hand,
letting the joyful spider the right fingers make
loose to spell and spell the thing she still can feel . . .

But not till decades later will she sense herself as music.
And what will bring her to it will be a need for solace
beyond the human kind.

# Vigil: Dwindle

—FOR MY FATHER

*Honor thy*
> *To thine own*
>> *Be of good*
>>> *Do no*

      but *harm* is already the background,
    a hum attuned, though we are not, to
the recent hue: his face becoming gradually blued

      the way, if you watch, in slow evening-time, distant
        mountains will somehow purple-up,

      but closer, like indigo velvet in the box
beneath his Navy Flying Cross,
      a little darkling sea in there, patriotic, roiling . . .

        Foiled, his hours
    trundle, lurch, or, more likely, creep

moss-slow. *Think* how that must feel
    —at sundown, say, stand in his room,
      cock your brain just so, and day

    ignites: through venetian blinds, a huge
doctor-headlamp in the face of all,

    the tunnel-end of all,
      the holy All we quailed at, formerly,
    but now, as the wrench of ownership pulls

his face from the lovelinesses he spent
    seven decades seeing, find

        we are going to face. About face:
    in the trawled-through afternoon's
minnowy, shadowy exigencies we say the names of

    mother, father, wife, daughter, daughter,
        and each one bounces off until

    his pillow is littered with family tree tinder
without which the brain's little scout-fire
        cannot even hope to start.

        For that is what His Cogency wants from us,
isn't it?

Warmth. Keep him warm. Light a fire.
    Kneel. Use the bellows. Blow.
        Again: Kneel. Bellow. Blow. Again:

# The Other Side

He drives her home like always
through the giant quiet dark-green patch of Central Park
in his tiny red car.

She still bleeds pretty badly, more than she'd expected
although she doesn't say so.
Neither wanted a child.

By now it's dim, 8 P.M.
Tall rows of tongue depressors
with orderly grids of illuminated teeth

—she knows that doesn't make sense—
prevent the ocean from flooding the park
—that doesn't make sense, either.

They have been to a building
behind whose windows were minutes,
about ten.

Now it is a good thing,
the red car like an emblem
not of the blood but of *what*?

There she is in the center
of millions and millions of people.
Of something fast and purposeful?

No one can touch her but him
and he doesn't want to now,
although he has been quite kind.

It is very quiet here.
There is the empty jogging trail
where she will jog again, a darker oval

worn into the green
that goes around a pond that is not
emptier than usual.

In three weeks' time
he will be gone
and the tiny significant red car

and the way it threaded through the public green
from his neighborhood to hers
and noticed the path and sped by it.

She will be on the other side
of childhood by then.
Half as old as I am.

A fox. That's red enough, a fox!
But, hunting or running away?
What, or away from what?

Her own life will have begun.

# Double Elegy in Spring

—FOR S.

Glove will do. Or foxglove.
The warm inside of missing them
or the trumpeting outside.

Here, here is a hand.
Sheathed and clutching a wild
belfry of pink throats—the wailing

not done, not yet.
But what kept you company: over.
What you measured your goodness by: gone.

And, worse, their recent narrow escapes:
that out from under the surgeon's saw
came the foot, still attached to your father,

that out from under years, no, fathoms
of booze, your friend's pickled leg nerves
twitched back;

so that now the two men
can walk toward you, invisibly,
dividing the distance between them

and you in half, in half, in half . . . .
You let out your end of the rope—
the casket's slight sway, your father

pushing you gently on the swing—
out and out till it thuds
on nothingness.

Useless, then,
before you toss it in, to pull the rope
toward you like a rake stuck in sodden leaves

wanting to clear an aisle for pure winter—
angle of rope like the sun's tilt
onto a hospital roof pad where that

same angle—why does everything
lean away from you?—of Styrofoam cooler's
metal handle to the heart inside gets

pureed by whirring
copter blade shadows—
You drop it. No one

could have used these hearts.
Your own feels dubious, flapping.
No way down

for your friend. No place for him
even in the earth, someone else got to decide,
just the mutterer's   *ashestoashestoashestoashes*   meanwhile

click and whir, some movie reel about
to show scenes from his boyhood?, so you
unbent your head, looked up through the thicket of hats and

caught sight of the little railway
tunneling into the silhouette of the ornate
fireplace, *that's*

what the marble thing was.
Then you walked outside and from
the high, gauche tower came the plume, yes, which meant

a new pope had been chosen, no, just
sickly smoke, dandruff-flecked, swarming with midges
—the Garden-of-Rest gardener relentlessly gardening,

stirring them up, was that it?—air
choking on itself and no one
saying so, no one arriving with nets, gas masks,

fine-toothed combs for anybody's hair, shovels for earth, for air—
just us standing around in our frumpy blacks,
us with our silly gloves and flopping flowers,

us, anyway, for you to be among,
strewn, as you were, across
inconsolable silence.

# The Swim

—FOR MY FATHER

He is so tired of being hauled up by the armpits.
    Dressed. Moved. Fed.

Tired of this parachute-feeling,
    day's long descent toward unfamiliar bed.

But the pool is waiting. The pool is always waiting.
    With its clear mood, with its doctor-smell chlorine.

There's a footpath to the edge that never dries, never.
    The air's nearsighted, blue.

He has earned the right
    to move among his species here,

legs successfully maneuvered
    into requisite florescent briefs.

Surely there's someone here
    who still needs him to hold *her*.

He reaches and reaches
    but nothing grabs back.

Not the swaddling water, not the fact
    that those dry strangers (us)

are waiting to take him home.
    Maybe—one moment in fifty?, like,

he is back on his lifeguard break
    flashing a few facile laps at poolside girls—

it is beautiful having
    no disbelief to suspend.

The brain floats in its case and the body floats after it.
    He hits the wall. Forgets. Aims for the other wall.

Here's how many laps he has swum:
    This one.   This one.

That is how God counts.

# The Composer

Fire sallies its plumes of yellow-orange,
    conveying matter to forever.
Cool ember who built it,
    I fuss with cantilevers.

After supper, the man with the young face
    wanted to know everyone's first loves.
Which made all the faces young.
    And put a flame into them.

Everyone has a story.
    His wife, barely thirty,
had died. And so his face
    glows unceasingly

either from his old love
    or from his new love
or from the alchemy between which is his life.
    An extra music in him.

Fire has something to tell.
    Listen: flags, rippling.
Up on the mainmast in stiff sleeves of wind.
    And crinkle of rain below, relinquishing extinguishing.

Sometimes we get our first loves.
    Sometimes we get our second loves.
Now, the last logs cave into a nestling.
    A high-pitched whine. A whistling. Diminishing.

# The Call

Two blocks from where the order beds at Kew
account for our vegetable beginnings,
underneath the garden's giant wooden flagpole,
pillar of dark in the dark
that crossed Nova Scotia stretched
between two logging trucks,
that nearly sank the ship it came on,
symbol of friendship between countries
that took the whole British army corps of engineers'
minds and bodies to hoist
so it could sport the flag on royal birthdays,

you sit in the flat we shared, its dark screenless windows
admitting the whole biting army of the invisible you have
to drop the phone every now and then to slap.

Sadness is your concert pitch, your A,
your affect, your affliction, your
abandoned form in its cave keeping warm
by the glow of figures on a screen

while the flagpole listens on into the dark,
poised against the shoulder of the bass violist
sleeping in his night-colored tux,
listens to the stirrings of the tousled flowers
resting from being looked at, waiting
for the virtuoso gardeners
to walk through the gate,
take up their gleaming hoes and rakes—

Everything in place like a birthday
the child awakens to too early,
the streamers still coiled in their coils,
the candles melting into one big year
in their flimsy box as dawn strikes them—

Everything that should be about the child
not about him yet,
maybe too late to ever be about him
now that he's glimpsed
magic's accouterments, is that what

our talking about it
across the ocean, our bodies shrunk
to sound waves in a thick black cord,
has done?

All winter long, when I was there to listen,
you read to me about Victor "the wild child"
and Jeanie, his wild sister in our century.
You made a study—their grunts, their lingering reliance
on all fours, their seemingly merciful
saviors and teachers who,
when celebrity cooled and government money
dried up at the frayed edge of their progress,
abandoned them to science, or silence.

Still, whether language is innate
obsessed you. How late in a life,
how far along, loping in the jungle or
tied to a potty chair in a silent room is too late

to learn the names of things,
to mix those sounds with other sounds
so what one desires can be asked for,
and someone of your same species might say, as I say,

yes. You in your temporary hermitage, yes.
You who grew up roaming open country
without rules or siblings, yes. You
whose language is an alien-sounding
brook I love, when I say *Please bring home
a book of British names*

I don't mean flowers' names, Latinate or common,
green or garish, clipped or shaped, shipped back
to the kingdom to be strolled through, studied,
trained to sprawl or articulate up lattices, one sample
of each—

I mean the name of our wildest idea,
the one we won't abandon
though oceans and trees don't need it,
though music goes on without it—

These weeks apart,
you seem to have drifted
back beyond wild to the wild,
but I still carry him in my strong mind
through fields of flowers,
as you will carry him in your strong arms
through fields of flowers,

and bring him here and tell him
how the idea of him (or is it a her?)
arose like a rose and found a way
to speak to us—never too late—near flowers.

# Interlude: February

Snow snows
within itself

time spends
time on

its little
blurry dinghy

ice is
installed in

blocks under
forehead flaps

or exudes
songs pointed

tear by
pointed tear

some days
it continues

some a
Baltic stasis

forgive the
cold world

I would
if I

could could
if wood

still green
inside could

say how
greenness understood.

# Opal

—TO THE UNBORN IN HURRICANE SEASON

Crazy rasta broccoli trees half
upon us, cool backyard shade

ground into the ground.
Poles swinging from wires

like bones from nerves.
Meaty atmosphere falling.

Lights going out, light going out, as
far from water water

circles. How do we prepare, presume?
They showed it on a show:

interpolated eye *in the socket of which*
the suave voice said *birds fly*

right through the glass screen
into the bowels of the TV

where it was blue, clear and clean,
chirpy as Miro. But here

the sky's so jammed with tears
no eye appears. Milky one, the world out here's

gone green, relentless green,
and I am caught like a baffle in between

you, future speller, and this green spell.
What did they tell me can be seen?

Omen-eye that ought to pass over,
tranquil-eye stuffed with bludgeoned birds,

eye on whose sight we spin
as if we were at the bottom of a drain

and come up gasping
in another hemisphere

brandishing something like your
eye-dot's red calm surrounded

by the havoc of our frantic
desiring and by the months-off future

where all all of us want
is to expel and love you?

Once, I was invisible.
They hadn't yet invented

the means for peering in.
Past, I love you, past

where an opal wrapped in bay leaf
made the wearer disappear.

First we're wrapped in fluids
and then the whole sky flushes them upon us—

days of this ahead—
the horrid pump pumps

like steel teeth on the steel
bread house, then the heave

of serum to the gutter like something long buried
that can't finish getting unburied,

Fire, Sun, Black, Precious, Noble *Opal,*
and we hadn't even thought of a girl's name yet.

# On Giving My Father a Book About Roses

Only child, he draws a child
upon a horse within a house upon a
—horse/house/hoarse—globby
thicket of graphite on graphite
piling up into a gawky rose

whose pistil the child lifts
—yellow pencil as thick as a horse's leg—
and draws that child who draws
that child who draws that
drawing child.

If he had had a brother
to remind him to move the pencil.
If he had had a horse, his own
large, large-eyed thing on whom

nothing is lost.
But that is what the rose is.
The rose on page one,
page one of the book
I gave him an hour ago.

Now he concentrates so hard
on this page he doesn't remember having seen
that the rose is a thicket of flesh-petals
breaking the tan soil of his brow.

And this hour spent talking of roses,
the one out in the trunk, concrete half of the gift,

of how we would plant it according to the book
on the sun-bleached side of his "assisted" dwelling . . .

You can have back this rose,
you big Universe Bud whose shuttlecock face
probes the dark interplanetary dirt.
You can have back the book, Cosmic Bookstore.

But when you excise this hour from his mind
—and me in that hour, and the small, coherent
splice of talk about roses—
I may not be able to forgive.

His face blooms scarlet,
his chin darts down for shade
as he has to ask my name

the way you have to re-ask the fancy names of roses
not because you weren't listening but because
you don't happen to have a head for roses.

How frightening to find,
an hour later, on your lawn
—an hour later than *what?*—
the splayed gloves, sharp-edged shovel, the
earth itself in a body-sized bag.

What
was somebody going to plant there
(did he plant me knowing what I was?)
and do I own up to the book about roses

now that the giving
rattles in his brain like an extra star
the ones who're science-smart, or dead,
already know *is* dead?

The drawn rose was always dead.
But it was the one that, pointing to the page,
we had agreed to plant.
I had agreed to plant.

May all the tiny grimbled-up lives
in this diatomaceous earth
shore up our storybook rose.
May its roots hoof out of their burlap sock,
may it raise up its apricot-blaze brain,

and may he remember what it is so he can water it,
or, if he can't,
may the rain remember to rain.

# Wolf Story

Our friends' boy, draped in the wolf,
will soon, we're sure, be draped in sleep;

the thick think-lines Magic-Markered on its brow
do all of his worrying for him.

The shirt is so big upon the essential boy
it makes a kind of tent of him, ghostly

except for the bite
where breath and brains periscope through.

He's safe. He comes
to get his goodnight kisses. Wolf,

he goes from one adult
house made of arms to the next.

But that is not the story.
The boy knows he is not the wolf,

not quite *that* beautiful to others,
though he does know—there's no word for it—just

the feeling of fur
from inside.

Under the coffee table lies
The Son of Big Chief Writing Pad

inscribed to this boy from this wolf
whose name is a river of jagged teeth

possibly discernible to scholars or mystics.
Below it, the boy is practicing *his* name,

but it is such a long way
from one letter-hill to the next.

You have to make a kind of inky trench
to the other sound *this* sound

can scramble over on, you have
to remember to double back

to drop the blobs
above the waiting stalks—though, look,

the *i*'s undotted—
maybe the boy can't go back.

The wolf is tired of hearing this stuff.
After its name, footprints

walk off the snowy page
that's riddled with actual chunks of shattered trees

—jungle, again, like where the wolf first appeared
to the boy's young father, drafted, dressed

to look like Vietnam itself,
before the boy was born.

It is an old wolf by now,
the father's imagination.

But it still takes on lupine form,
and it still knows its fierce one-syllable name

suitable as a battle cry but pronounceable
for stateside use (inscribed on the wolf's own napkin holder),

though I will not write it here. It has not yet been
my privilege to learn it directly from the boy

who does not yet suspect the written word
broadcasts your secrets like tracers. So that

they look at you then, the whole stuffed
dinner party contingent bloated

with new knowing as you,
inside the beautiful, oversized, flowing

body of the wolf that even
bad mall art can't maim, say

*Goodnight, goodnight everybody*, getting
the rounds of hugs dropped all over you,

picking up camp with your wolf, its pads, your pad,
going up to your room, no big deal,

and now your father, the one who came back alive,
goes after you to read you

some bedtime story that *is*
the story.

# The Seventh Day

His guise, gaze, was still, or already,
that of a creature who roams
or else is tired of roaming

and so it mattered not
that his father had selected
two lovelinesses of this world to be his:

one bear, blue as scotch
or Scotch Ice, and one set
of doll clothes that fit.

Nor that we would smuggle him out of the blinding room
of trays arranged like a picnic or a butcher shop
—the one-lb. club, the two-, the three- —

at midnight having first washed the car
as there was nothing else to wash and it seemed
to want to be part of the story, gray, spotty, almost a horse,

and him in two hats like a prince
or a little man selling hats
or a refugee wearing both hats

and already mouthing his part
—fur still covering the face, I swear, I have a picture;
ears still stationed by the mouth, I swear, I have a picture—

in the story of the dark wood and the thing
(we could hear the footsteps inside him)
that needed (that never got closer) to be found.

Then suddenly they peeled off
the shiny plastic hearts that had, from the beginnng,
held the reins to his heart

and the screen which was the story of his life
went dark and he turned
and started guzzling the silence.

# Sylvia's Starlings

Today's cool, quite un-sun, but
sung about by mouths
for whom a collection is being taken up:

$3.75 per plastic tub of worms.
Limp noodles, old rice, wet cat food, nothing
quiets them like worms.

And make sure the dirt's still on them: roughage.
And do it even though they're common: starlings.
And don't forget to go into that room every hour

and unhinge the cat cage
the cat is outside of, unhang
the doily, the tea towel, the dread . . .

There are yellow mouths in there!
Two broken egg yolks!
Worms now! Little forceps! How small

a thing is worth
getting up in the middle of the night for,
and what about two small things, does that make it

twice as noble? You, common animal, with your
five fingers, each of which is plumper than their
two necks combined, look

at how big the powers of giving are, picture your hand
from their point of view: how
unfeathery, what precise oafs we are, look at

the fat bait shop man
sunk back in the green nest
of our soft dollar bills,

look at our heroic names
recorded on the envelope of money marked
"Worm Fund for Board Members Leonard and Jill":

this is a test of our silliness,
which one will actually put her hand
into the gaudy maw;

this is a test of who's scrawnier, uglier,
this is the Wright brothers—ah, two of them!—
let's take pictures, let's build our hopes on them, this is the big deal

wind-in-branches story in which
the hero parts the icy waters I mean licey feathers
en route to the promised land;

this is a test of how much we need the fallen,
this is the question the winds asks and
this is two answers the cat gives

if we give up at all.

# Ark

They came from behind a curtain
onto the dream's dry land.
One of everything this time,
paired with its silhouette.

The elephant small as a burnished nickel.
All the others smaller, but elephant-colored,
as if the curtain had done that,
the elephant-paint still wet.

The path they made, noses to tails,
a giant, backward S, the way a child will draw it,
still looking out from inside the alphabet.
Plural, but not something meaning something.

Then, as always,
they went back up the ramp,
everything I loved
before I loved the alphabet.

Suddenly, the baby trumpeted from this world   *I! I! I!*
and brought me to the crib gate: one of him, too!
But pink, a color this side
of disaster. Thank you.

# The Primary Tool Is Soup

Out of the quiet, someone.
　　No, two someones.

Two oranges presiding on the sill.
　　Phone goes. Friends ill.

But we were just now thinking how the maple on the hill
　　held still, remember? And held the wind inside it—

The mind is a sieve. Things drain. Or won't.
　　No that's the body. No that's the mind.

Insanity. Cancer.
　　Soup. Here—.

Something in them *could* be maple-red? Well.
　　And boot-heel red, as the boot is lifted

from the face, mind's
　　body-meal revealed—

Rhyme, old refuge.
　　Time, old appeal.

Orzo. Orzo. Ergo,
　　tomato.

A second nurse must also check for blood in the tubing.
　　Liability's red. No, green.

Inside, the oranges must be made of china.
  Or we could put our fingers through. All the way to China.

Put it on the calendar.
  Pumpkin treatment. Leek.

Everyone says the right thing.
  Grinds their teeth in sleep.

What grinds words to salve?
  Her son designs things hospitals have.

Don't talk about language.
  The primary tool is soup.

Oranges pocked with doubt
  but ringed with warm blue fur.

What makes wildness safe?
  Quick-draw blood-draw thing.

Sun, like an orange, above us . . .
  And parasols smeared with lace . . .

Never again mock oranges.
  Seventeen days withdrawal from mock oranges.

"In my dream I took the old mind of one
  and the young body of—"

Wildness is chemical.
　　Wildness is treatable.

"In my dream I gave them the oranges,
　　for scurvy—"

Wilderness is beatable.
　　Wildebeest is eatable.

One unbearably old looking. One just unbearable.
　　To themselves.

Neither one can sleep so they both have access
　　to the magic hours. Rabbits, rabid . . .

Mulligatawny. Reheat the Fibonacci-Fern.
　　Plain Ole Carrot. Fish (burned).

Their wildnesses must be so
　　*disappointed.*

Orange seed-size
　　word for it.

Two sets of teeth clacker down the stairs.
　　Stop. *Eat.*

The primary tool is soup.
　　Getting hard to touch them with our hands like shining ladles.

E-mail travels like blood.
    Yes. They're alive.

Oranges on the other hand. Matter
    of interpretation. Soup on the other hand.

One is going to the forest to be healed.
    Wild mushroom with wild turnip dice.

One is bound in the forest of her house.
    Chicken and rice and everything nice.

The primary tool is soup. The primary tool is soup.
    Mercy tastes like iron. The primary tool is soup.

# Moment of Brain

brain says   This thing That thing
brain says   All I wanted

All I wanted! All I wanted . . .
brain, tired, says Things

curtain star sun
curtained scissored sunned

sunfish on starboard a light you can see through if you put your face in
stars starfish fishstars

brain says   Long day
brain says   The elemental hypothesis

Who's there in the murk?
With his wet chalkboard?

purloined link hinky dink
one curvaceous two curvaceous

whompa lob lob lob lob lob
Whomp   Whoops

TV says   Manymany love
brain says   Ina ina box, fox

inedible brightness   Gag
till someone walks in   Flip

Wherever Is is is
wherever brain is

Is is tired
but Lie or Lay which is it, Is?

# Elegy for the Difference Between Reading and Being

Someone's writing, in a book,
that had the word *mortal* before
the word *splendor* and said it was
what someone said about someone
who received it like a wafer—

it didn't say *wafer* but that was what she thought,
something famous, nourishing, religious, dissolving,
she who decided from that
moment onward to be *she*,
self-at-a-distance you could put
where you wanted, her arm
through whosoever arm, whichever sleeve
or window,

for someone's written words
had made her that sad. The permanent,
obstinate, drowning, indelibly sad *sad thing*
that was now detached from words.

And the space all around her?
—hardly a space compared
to the book's field of stars.
Mottled napkin, sad stick of wood
still wet with stirring something long drunk,
and her mind, unquiet, or, unhinged, hugely so,
compared to the minds in the book.
It made her heart big
—it actually pinched in its cage—
and the book made no place for her heart.
Not between its covers or its words.

How *something* art is.
And her small son always saying
I want to be *in* there, the picture book
open in their laps, and her always saying, So what
would you do if you *were* in there?
and hating how that satisfied him.

Her friends had hated, last month,
how the poet whose last book
was about life had read aloud instead
from the new one about words.
And she had agreed, not being able
to hear the note of grief inside it
that *was* it.

Now came the time when she heard.

# The Scientist

Certain snails, pale ones,
high on the stone wall
get $x$ hours of sun.
Others, darker, lower down, $y$ hours.

He likes the bench very much.
How, from here, his mind can put
any four together
—little, big, pearly, brown—

like a pair of mismatched shoes
waltzing with a partner
slowly swept without her
knowing off her feet.

What if love *were* this possible
all over, why not, the world?
Back in the lab this morning, the beautiful dark
woman from Bosnia lost in her latest letter—

her father, a surgeon, almost finished
going blind, the simple drug's name
still left off the Red Cross list—
never looked up from the minefield studded

with beakers, pipettes.
But what if, next to the purposive shapes
of his muscular hands
and bright surgical instruments,

that father-darkness
is growing at a rate which bears
some correlation to how fast the woman's
dark face has been darkening

—color of olives, the sun
going down in the olives—
lately—how long now?—
and one could take note, also, of how

sadness becomes her,
and escapes . . . . He stares. Science
requires his passivity.
Spiral.  Spiral.  Glide.

Suck.
Ooze.
Nothing about his body
is like their bodies.

A triangle sturdy enough to steady
an easel or a camera on
spans snails and the snail-
hypothesis and him.

He leans a little closer—which one is she?—
and leaf-shadow stipples him:
pale snails clinging to the white envelope
deep—he knows this—in the bottom of her purse,

that pallor dotted with the darkness
of the ones on the bottom
closing the father's eyes with the cool
tongues of their bodies for good.

Nothing's ever happened to him
that could make her love him.
All poetry did was speckle him like a trout.
But $x$, rhapsodic $x$, the full sun shining upon her

says:
Light one, got it? Dark one.
Big one. Little one.
Slowly now.   Left foot and   right foot and . . .

# Elegy for Lessons

When I have reached the point of no return, I return
    to the girl and her indelible mascara of sadness
that came from her knowing her fate
    and the words for her fate, but not
the rhythm of the words, not
    the dance inside them, when I recall

her strength that had nowhere to go,
    that chewed upon itself like a bone,
like a muscle chewing on its own bone,
    that knows the taste of chalk inside, but not
what can be written, not what will not
    wash off, when I follow

the string of time back
    to where it splays into five lines
full of notes someone else
    has written, and watch her lift the finger
of the flute and point it
    away from the page, when I hear

her try to proclaim
    in a language crowded with tone and tones
and rhythm, yes, and pure flying, yes,
    and dancing, yes, and shape-in-air but not
the *what* or *who* or *why* or *where*
    of the life inside it, when I see her

on her bicycle trolling
    the vicinity of her flute teacher's house
because, after all, he has told her

she must exercise her lungs,
the bicycle itself like three flutes
    lashed together, when I smell

the omen-odor of diesel fuel
    flare up and feel the truck mirror sever
her handlebar an inch
    from the finger that works
the flute A-flat key or typewriter *a*
    if she survives, when I think

of her face rising moon-slow in the ditch
    to shine across the field into the back room
in that house where music
    and kindness were boiled and distilled
once, unbearably once,
    in the crucible of the body, when I feel

her resurrect herself
    thumb by gear by hair, tube by
wind by limb into a whole girl dizzy
    in the rank ranks and haze
of towering, terrifying corn,
    once, just once, let me say:

    *You've had a long ride filled with longing*
*but you can brush yourself off now,*
    *the blood and grease are only*
*blood and grease and you still have*
    *ten fingers you can fashion into*
*something or other that flies,* when I see

myself look back then as at
    a house on fire, no shoulder left
to lean on, go ahead and say that,
    no shoulder left to lean on,
boy's or man's or road's,
    then, in the corn, it's there:

power:
    the chain-linked, buzzing, bolted city of volts
from which the nerves branch to the populus.
    Behind, in the ditch, the fire music is.
And unspoken misery thereunto pertaining.
    Ahead, some sort of life among people.

The only way out is to marry the source of power
    or to move in the direction of its uses on the earth.

# Patton Lake

—FOR MY SON AT TWO


The mud flats stink like sun-cracked haunches of dead horses.
How long it takes to die, which battle, they won't say.

We count survivors: Conestoga mailbox, inlet jammed with turtles,
swarms of invading three-pointed kudzu stars.

First I'm diving uphill, flat-out, pushing the stroller,
one hand down on your cheek, the awning yawning

green unto collapse above our heads,
then it's time for you to put your full-grown hand

to my cheek at the end or a little before the end.
Whatever's in between

will someday be dead horses who won't know
they were petted or that, tonight, the moon

almost came all the way down in, or into,
this our life. It's time to go.

But you say, once more, *roundaroundaround!*
For this is the hour of flowers

furling up petals, of kudzu's groggy rocking
in the hard-soft hammock of its *u*'s.

Hour when the ducklings—recently, utterly, disappeared—
might shine up through the murk—

If ever all the animals are gone from you,
the farm set bare and the word you need to name

the stall door's rattle
—house- or thimble-sized, hay-scarred, horrible—

is one I took with me
or one I never said,

remember golden ducklings
could be coins in a fountain,

or lovely yellow streetlights under a turtle sky,
or the *Red-Blue-Yellow-Shoe* yellow

of the yellow thing the first time you said yellow—
Anything is beautiful

or anything is something else
and that thing, then, is beautiful

or something that is something that is
something that is beautiful.

Bury the language with me
that kept me, afternoons, from you.

Take what's left around.
Sing what's left: a round.

# Interlude: Still Still

Inside the hole, where it's yellow,
the boy has dropped a quarter
so that the guitar rattles

when he shakes it by the neck.
Knocks, scrapes, scars.
So this is what music is.

The wooden body is no longer
bigger than his body.
The strings, which, when

he strums them,
go on forever, are forever
wound around small pegs

shaped like the big ones
they wrap the ropes around,
there being an absence of

able-bodied mourners
to lower, with the softer machines
of their bodies, the coffin down.

It was a cold day.
The boy had not been born yet,
but stood among us

warm in his round place.
Then, from the distance,
the bagpiper who'd been found

in the yellow pages
extracted the horizon note
like a red needle from the sky.

And so it was not with nothing
human our friend was lowered.
This is what music is.

But how did it sound to the boy,
the bladder of cries squeezed
through the slit throat

when there had not been anything
yet to cry about?
The solace of music is

not that we recognize it.
It is that the hearing
comes from before and is wound

around after. Between,
our bad singing a stranger
dozed, then bulldozed to.

At home, in its case, the guitar
was hunkered inside the dark
into which music goes,

and the more particular dark
from which music comes
was inside of it.

The sound hole swallowed and passed back
buckets of silence
until the inner and outer dark

had the same yellow smell.
This, while the song the boy
would pay for waited, still still.

# Ballad in Fall

Dear, green branch,
    bereft as earth in space,
squeezing a little oxygen
    from a futile blue place,

how can I renege?
    The red man already stands
aloft in the picker and revs
    the furious smile in his hands.

For you—or what's not you,
    to which you are attached—
have passed from green to dead.
    Summer, your match.

I swear I believe in red.
    Three months, I'm gone. Now this.
I'm back for fall to fell
    what became of bliss.

I said I believe in red,
    what dies should gradually die.
In colors you can't turn
    my father's parched lips lie

open these long years.
    A mouth, incised and red,
delivers pale brown gruel.
    Just certain parts are dead.

My job is to stand by
    three hundred yards, or miles.
I dream of pails of water
    limbs and lips revile.

I dream it in full color.
    I dream it in rushing sound
to cover the chest-rattling, scream-
    inside-it thing that's all around;

I dream it brimming over.
    I dream it anyway.
I dream a furious brigade
    of red, red leaves that say

it's best to fall in the fall,
    to gradually go.
Red is the color of God's eyes.
    Beautiful, no?

# Whether or Not There Are Apples

—FOR D.

I like to take the dress off the line,
the heat still in it.
The heat comes from the whole dress into me,
and the smell of apples,
whether or not there are apples.
It comes into me it comes into me it solves
a simple coldness.
All these years I still unpin you from the air
when I feel the other, unfathomable, cold.
You are your same shape
and weightless as a photograph
and I can find you any old where, my darling, my
direction. There is a moment when the heat is finally
gone out of the dress so that
it disappears till I think *dress*
and then it's there, and spent.
It is like the little dead space, blue hinge
at the switchback of breathing.
Then the dead air comes out.
Every time I've needed you you
let me dress in your old soul and smell you.
Since you died I've taken you,
I've taken you in, just in.
But I am getting old.
And so I need to ask you.
Maybe I'll be able to cross
the quick blue shift without you.
But will you be wanting to take me
in colorless windrows of wind
instead of my long brown hair?

# On Thursday She Began Saying Everything at Once

On Thursday she began saying everything at once
but her heart had a problem keeping up
so she took a bow tie and a half of the drug
which slowed her to where she could
speak out loud again but it fogged in

her brain so she knew then she would have to
live always in fog the way the citizens do
in Seattle where she'd once scanned
the ledges of mist, truly lost. The words there
were a mist and the thing to say

a bell buoy far offshore, ridiculous
to her in her raincoat whose lining
was secretly green as the sea where the only light
comes from the foreheads of surgeon fish
sulking and stalking the ledges,

as has been mentioned, of mist.
She hates that the onrushing
and also the blood-letting language
that mops up and maps the top layer
of dream is made out of the same words

we use to buy fish. Others have praised
this condition for centuries but she has always
hated it—like Mozart pumped into the fishmonger's
briny speakers, beautiful scales shorn, hacked, slimed
to scales upon a scale.

What you do, she decided on Thursday, is
go on. Move forward. Swim. Like a fish. Or die. You go:
*Here I come.* You go: *Give me a break.*
You decide that the words can listen
for once and pour *you* a cup of the coffee the

whole city will get famous for before
it becomes Thursday outside words
and the coffee an excuse to condense oneself
to saying something *suave* to someone *suave*
about some very *suavey* thing in a language

you speak just one word of: *grande.*
The consequence of which makes your heart race, bad.
And so you double up, two whole bow ties like a ballplayer
hefting two bats who's about to smack open the bleachers' screams
of nothing other, and nothing, and other, than all the words at once.

# Slide

Slide the top jaw right,
*teeth tooth troth*
now slide the lower jaw left.
*beast feast trash*
Notice the hills and valleys
*garbage barage age*
on the overhead screen.
*age stage maid*
If you continue to grind
*calendar lender door*
your teeth   any   more
*moor mar mur mur*
if you keep on, especially
*zzz*
at
*zzz*
night we shall have to keep on doing
*oar our room rouse*
root canals which you
*do the do   move   vroom*
of course don't
*gladiolas glad violas not one iota*
want. Listen.
*lalalalalalalala*
You must look
*hookcookbook   looseSeuss*
for more suitable means
*meanie!   meaning?*
by which
*I . . . O . . .   itch!*
to express your

*Slide, abide. What's said inside,*
*behind the mouth's closed door,*
*needs to say and hide*
*itself. Nothing more.*
Have you considered another
    *veer wind sheer fear*
career? It's black and white
    *checker-player soda-jerker cow-milker*
as that.
    *Sat. Sad. Mad.*
Lean back now. Recline.
    *hack hack   blind*
Don't mind the lead apron.
    *Don't, mind. (The led ape ran.)*
Stop bruxing.
    *Buxom brush!*
Remember not to grind.
    *But there's a mill that isn't so*
Try to relax as you sleep.
    *and death comes, certain nights, too slow—*
Questions? I'll refer you to
    *sweet speech-sprockets, lumbering tongue, neither un- nor done*
someone. A clinic.
    *quickclick licklick nitpick chicksick*
For help.
    *Yelp.*

# Her Job

She wanted to be alone.
Then more alone, in public.
So she began to haunt the coffeehouse,
ordering a small cup and retiring
to a small table by the back window
with her many notebooks.
And the coffee would go down the pipe
of her throat, the equal and exact
opposite of music. And make
a hot blank path:
                        her own interior
glance like a wasp
that decides on you and loses
its strength in you as it
flies away—or does it die, then,
ask the book, the long-ago book—
either way, full of blood
the stinging part can't have.
                        When the hour
was up she'd go back to her life,
click, click, the hip flexors lifting her
                        but first
she would dismantle the outside world
by looking at it through the window,
church brick rectangle by church brick rectangle
to see the thing behind, beyond, board
fitting board, then steel beam by sweat by stroke down
to the blueprints, she could never get the blue out
where someone claimed that air.

                         All she needs
is a few square thousand miles,
and she knows if she could find this space
outside to accommodate all of the inside,
then when her own brain
starts flaking to ash there will be a place
to be wheeled in
                         that will feel familiar.
This job of finding
a suitable place for the inner life
before it is too late is her most important job
but the child musn't know it, ever.
And so she would go home, then, to the child.

## Ancient New Parents

No one likes to mention the gate of eternity.
No one likes to say they stood there so long

the hinges acquired the eyelids' creak.
Nor how the half-life of haggardness tarries.

Nor how tardiness tarnishes, triples, or tears
an arm off miracles,

nor how long speechlessness lasts,
nor how the best name got squandered on the dog.

No one says how books you're meant to read aloud
say *safe*, well and good, but *from a watery grave*,

and *I'm not going to do Nothing any more*
and *well, not so much, they won't let you*

and then *he was silent again*, though you know
he kept bringing half the earth in in a shoe.

So let it be said,
little grease monkeys, distant astronauts,

whom we may need to fix us
or help us leave the earth,

your first raiments, at least,
were whole, almost seamless,

and footed, and one had tiny wings;
and soft, and quick to change

like a sky. Like distance. Like the distant,
extant, accelerating vista.

# To Brain on Brain's Last Day as Brain

Svelte sphere,
    smelling, smelting, fear;

fusing what you used
    to do—*fish/flash*—

with what's
    relentlessly near

which is the same as "here"
    which is the same as "ear" and "mere":

Dear one, listen here:
    It's just

the glow of words
    boiled down to sound:

a *you* crooning to a *you*
    in some chosen ground.

At tunnel's, barrel's, end,
    not light but *this*:

rivers and dendrites
    tuned and twanged,

sticky-sweet, thickly
    blissed and glissed . . .

Meanwhile, certain
    maps collapse.

But now, at last,
    let the band begin.

You, if you're ready,
    fall right in.

# On Being Asked About Giving Up the Flute

It will be four o'clock
when I find a way to go back over into music.
Four o'clock or in 4/4 and I'll say

I'll take that, that basic
six-disc changer, just install it
in the trunk because one ought not to see

the place music comes from, especially ought not
to snap back the eyelid and handle,
while driving, God's—don't put your thumbs on it—brain.

Just drive, windows up.
Just loll wholly over.
Private music's best, most like

the little alien standing on a mountainside,
earphones stretched around the little
oval of his head, volume off, listening

to sheep weep.
Heitor Villa-Lobos once sketched
the New York skyline's undulations

then laid a staff across it
to hear it for what it was.
But, malcontent

with the twisted cathedrals of my ears,
for years *I* tried to *play*,
like a spider feeling

the silk pass out of it
and gliding on it and knowing it shows off
the feeling and the gliding,

the score of some ravishing vanishing.
His duet from *Bachianas Brasileiras*, for example,
I liked to play the flute part

while a virtuoso kid named Herbert,
what a minefield of a face, played the bassoon
so well he could sightread back through time

from skyline girder down to the last dotted sheep
as if he'd tended it from birth
with his whole doomed, puckered life,

and sweep me up, broom and swoon,
two thousand feet back up.
What if this new century

is only going to be about longing
for old longing? I would like to drive back
while I still have time to where the curve

of Herbert's and Heitor's young brows above the
closed eyes above the sucked-in lips
is all I know of beauty.

I would not glance in the rearview to the future.
I would but ride the cascade back
to my original, deafening intents . . .

—Cowardly, this beauty
of forms without words
words cannot help but want.

Do you have six copies, please, of this particular disc?
Six habitable planets to circle my new sun?
It's four o'clock, concert time, and I'm going to play the first one,

and if it should make me feel banished,
cast-off, star-stunned, drifting,
I'm going to play the second one,

and if it should make me feel banished,
cast-off, star-stunned, drifting,
I'm going to play the third one,

and if it should make me feel banished,
cast-off, star-stunned, drifting . . .

# The Difference Between Writing and Music

She is walking out of the city
—reader, it is your city—
she is walking away from them, the mangled
hem of her dress slogging in them,
leaving a pattern like wingbeats stuck in them,
but walking anyway although
every moment she doesn't look back
is bound to accelerate their . . .
Huh? Who?
She has outdistanced their fingerprints, voiceprints,
the dampness of their bodies, the slick slide of
their words on hers, and that
it is beautiful around her—
the city lights like multicolored candies
thrown against her black dress—
is, now, hindrance, annoyance, no chance.

The only beauty she wants now
is something durable—more than the languor of suspect sentences
trailing from her mouth like scarves—
she wants something to keep in her purse,
Lucite dandelion paperweight, maybe something like that,
the only thing her father has
that is beautiful and his in the end,
a delicate, illegible dispersing, that's all she wants,
crossing, now, the scraggly band of wasteground circumnavigating
this city with its belt of no-hope, its dispossessed's
trust I mean truss, a dusty bracelet she has to slip out of,
past shredded tires, amputated motors, amputated dolls
punctuated, punctured with what looks like
that beautiful weed but don't

mistake it, don't go asking whose doll it was,
who drove her where, who put it into words. She
will soon have all she wants, her trusty unassailable
cube of beauty that no one can tangle a story
up in since all the notebooks
you can buy in this city come from the chain of shops that
now sell mostly greeting cards, dear Mummy,
dear John, on the occasion of your
umpteenth, congrats, oh *sorry*, all of the notebooks
she bought here were embellished with the gaunt suffering
face of the famous woman writer,
*so*
the face said, *you can do words or have*
*happiness, one or the other, kiddo*
whilst inside, of course: blank: the famous face
just as it was born, a moment
before the cry that divided her,
two moments before arms involved her, and bound,
no choice, with brash green wire, emaciated
garter snake spiral. So. She,
like she said,
is walking out of your city now,
out of this world, out of the way of words
equaling anything, past the periphery, beyond
circumference, off the edge, over the hill, out to where
the glinting stars are women picking up their flutes and saying:

# Postlude for Penny Whistle, Spoons, and Drum

I've heard it spoken of as the other side
    as if it were a record to flip over.

I've heard it called a gate
    as if there were a creak and then a creek

and then a bridge and then they lie, say you will lie
    amid flowers instead of sores,

and levitate, as now, but there will be
    no harness . . .

They don't speak of the weather.
    They never speak about the weather

or whether anyone misses anyone
    there. Or is it *then*.

Here, summer. God-awful.
    Too hot to tuck the boy in.

Books stuck to the shelf.
    Thinking ripening its own intolerable self.

The boy's big question still unasked.
    Unasked, and, so, unanswered, as,

night after night, story after story,
    mild after milder terror unfolds.

Read to me at the end if there is time.
    And if I fail to understand read to me anyway.

While I'm still flesh and bits of sound,
    let my son say some sentences over me,

structures like this room, whole houses
    that will house what we read

long ago. And let the air arrange itself
    the way a flute will sometimes arrange the dust

into the spine of a tree
    and the branches of a woman and a man.

Above me, in the ground,
    several works to weigh me down.

No one needs to read them.
    They'll change back to sound.

Or, if I am returned to air I shall, sometimes and
    sometimes, be his confidant who loved him beyond bearing it—

This, on a night the heart wears thin
    and the medicine does no good.

This, on a night the brain wears thin
    and the medicine does not exist.

My son knows not how to read.
　　His grandfather forgot.

But let it be recorded
　　how each, in his time, loved soup.

And chomped his teeth into the spoon.
　　And how, in the months leading up to

or in the slow years leading down from
　　his time of eating soup,

each stirred at the stir of words
　　and cried back what sounded sometimes

like music and sometimes like a burning
　　scraped from the bottom of song.


—ROBERT HENRY BEHN, 1919–2001

"Still Life": The italicized lines owe a debt to Deborah Digges's poem "Sycamores" in *Late in the Millennium*. Her lines read "Before you can let go / there is this last terrible embracing."

"The Call": Kew Gardens, London.

"The Seventh Day": Brookwood NICU, Birmingham, Alabama.

"The Primary Tool Is Soup": In memory of Shirley Musgrave.

"Elegy for the Difference Between Reading and Being": The appellation "mortal splendor" appears in "The Seventh Night," in Robert Hass's *Sun Under Wood*.

"The Scientist": The image of the intent study of snails is drawn from Piaget's early investigations into the classification of mollusks in Neuchâtel, Switzerland.

"Ancient New Parents": The italicized lines are from *Madeline* and *Winnie the Pooh*.

"On Being Asked About Giving Up the Flute": Thanks to Lisa Peppercorn, Villa-Lobos's biographer, for details about his methods of composition.

## THE BRITTINGHAM PRIZE IN POETRY

The University of Wisconsin Press Poetry Series · Ronald Wallace, General Editor

### PLACES /EVERYONE
Jim Daniels · C. K. Williams, Judge, 1985

### TALKING TO STRANGERS
Patricia Dobler · Maxine Kumin, Judge, 1986

### SAVING THE YOUNG MEN OF VIENNA
David Kirby · Mona Van Duyn, Judge, 1987

### POCKET SUNDIAL
Lisa Zeidner · Charles Wright, Judge, 1988

### SLOW JOY
Stephanie Marlis · Gerald Stern, Judge, 1989

### LEVEL GREEN
Judith Vollmer · Mary Oliver, Judge, 1990

### SALT
Renée Ashley · Donald Finkel, Judge, 1991

### SWEET RUIN
Tony Hoagland · Donald Justice, Judge 1992

THE RED VIRGIN: A POEM OF SIMONE WEIL
Stephanie Strickland · Lisel Mueller, Judge, 1993

THE UNBELIEVER
Lisa Lewis · Henry Taylor, Judge, 1994

OLD AND NEW TESTAMENTS
Lynn Powell · Carolyn Kizer, Judge, 1995

BRIEF LANDING ON THE EARTH'S SURFACE
Juanita Brunk · Philip Levine, Judge, 1996

AND HER SOUL OUT OF NOTHING
Olena Kalytiak Davis · Rita Dove, Judge, 1997

BARDO
Suzanne Paola · Donald Hall, Judge, 1998

A FIELD GUIDE TO THE HEAVENS
Frank X. Gaspar · Robert Bly, Judge, 1999

A PATH BETWEEN HOUSES
Greg Rappleye · Alicia Ostriker, Judge, 2000

HORIZON NOTE
Robin Behn · Mark Doty, Judge, 2001